ALLEN PHOTO

C000245865

ALL ABOUT LONG REINING

CONTENTS

Long reining requires skill and tact but a higher standard of training can be achieved with long reining than with lungeing. Before you introduce the horse to the long reins make sure he is obedient to the lunge aids, particularly the voice aids for halt, walk, trot and canter. Always lunge him before you begin every long-reining session. The novice long reiner is advised to practise the open-rein method until experience is gained. With this method the long reins run directly from the bit rings to the trainer's hands which is more akin to lungeing. If anything goes wrong, therefore, the handler can regain control as they would when lungeing; this is not so easy to do when the reins run through the D rings.

TACKING UP

THE ROLLER

Select a roller with D ring attachments. The choice of Ds attached at different heights allows you to position the reins to suit the needs of each individual horse.

Alleviate pressure points on the horse's back by placing a numnah under the roller.

THE CAVESSON AND BRIDLE

A cavesson padded with soft leather prevents chafing. Ensure the jowl strap is tightened sufficiently because this stops the cheek straps slipping over the horse's eyes and face.

The noseband must fit well above the horse's nostrils so he can breathe freely. Place the cavesson straps under the bridle cheek pieces.

THE BIT

A cheeked snaffle prevents the bit from slipping through the horse's mouth.

PAUL'S TIP

A French link bit with keepers and cheeks helps guide the horse by acting against the horse's face. The cheeks also avoid the bit being pulled through the horse's mouth when he is turning.

THE SADDLE

A saddle can be used in place of a roller. To introduce the horse to the long reins, tie both stirrups down with string: knot one end of the string around the left stirrup, run it over the girth and secure it with another knot to the right stirrup. The long reins can then be run through the stirrup irons.

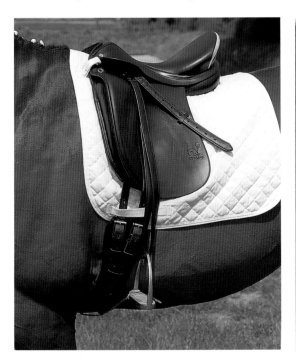

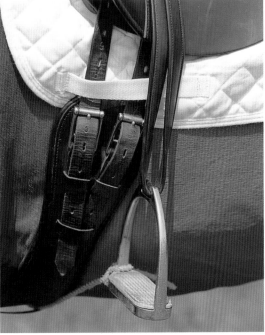

This is the traditional English method of long reining.

PAUL'S TIP

Follow safety measures: wear a hard hat and gloves and always position yourself a safe distance from the horse's hindquarters.

THE LONG REINS

The long reins should be approximately 25 ft (8 m) long. They are made of rope or cotton web. Make sure they feel well balanced and light in your hands.

PAUL'S TIP

Avoid nylon reins. They are much more likely to give rope burns and can also burn the horse's sides. Always wear gloves. They prevent rope burns if the horse pulls the reins through your hands.

Use soft long reins, they flow easily through the stirrup irons or D rings.

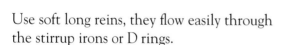

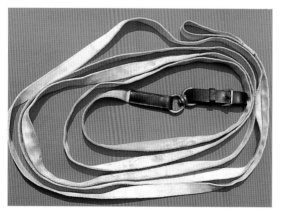

New reins can be fluffed up and made to feel 'older' by washing them in conditioner.

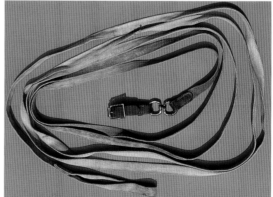

STEP-BY-STEP

STEP 1

Coiling the reins Coiling the reins is vital to successful long reining. It enables you to maintain light and balanced hands while changing direction. Take the time and make the effort to master the techniques.

Use the outside hand to coil up several lengths of inside rein and coil up several lengths of the outside rein with your inside hand. (Inside and outside refers to left and right. The inside is the side of the horse nearest to you, i.e. the side from which you would lunge the horse.)

Continue to coil the inside and outside reins in sequence until you are close to the horse.

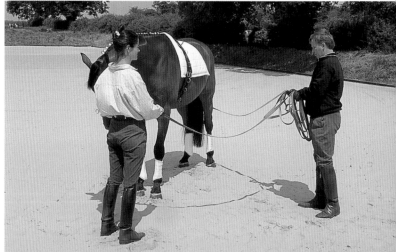

STEP 2

Introduce the second, or outside, rein The horse should already be used to one long rein, i.e. the lunge rein so, introduce the second rein when you feel sure the horse will willingly and calmly accept it lying over his back. Observe his reactions and if he remains calm you can move onto the next stage of placing the outside rein.

Initially, attach the long reins to the cavesson. If you attach the reins to the bit before you are competent enough to handle the reins and stay with the horse's movement you could spoil the horse's mouth.

Attention to detail

Improve your long-reining techniques by paying attention to small details. For example, in this photograph, a rein is snagged under the numnah. If this happens, replace the outside rein, and only then move on to the next stage.

Placing the outside rein

Place the outside rein over the croup. Be careful to leave the rein slack from the croup to the horse's head and check that this slack does not fall over his tail.

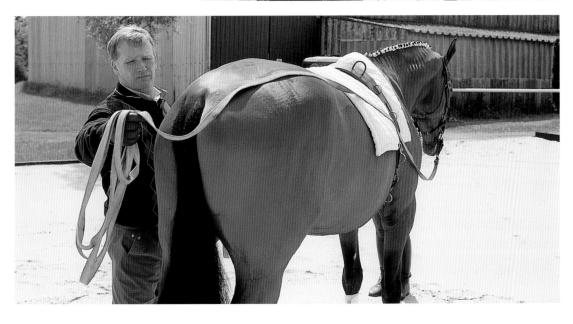

Moving off Slide the outside rein down the horse's buttocks and rest it above and around his hocks. This rein simulates the rider's outside leg and controls the quarters.

Practise Step 2 for approximately 1–2 weeks and progress to Step 3 only when the horse:

a. works equally well on both reins on a large circle;

b. is obedient to the aids;

c. is confident and happy to accept the long reins.

PAUL'S TIP

Be careful not to over-tighten and pull the outside rein thus causing it to get caught under the horse's tail which would probably frighten him.

You should practise the open-rein method of introducing and changing the rein at the walk, and only progress to the faster gaits when you are skilled at coiling and uncoiling the reins.

The assistant's role The assistant is there to pat and calm the horse while you begin teaching him new techniques.

STEP 3

Changing the rein on the move Practise this new movement in walk before you progress to the faster gaits. Walk the horse forwards and ask him to follow the line of an S shape (when he changes the rein on the move, the horse's hoof prints draw this letter on to the arena surface). Plan each part of the S shape before you direct the horse to move around it and you will find the exercise flows easily.

Move one Change the rein from left to right. Begin the movement by walking the horse on the left rein.

Move two Walk behind him at a 45 degree angle and ask him to step well into a corner of the school. The school walls help prepare him to start the S shape and discourage him from speeding up.

Move three Coil up several lengths of the left rein with the right hand.

Move four Ask the horse to walk towards the straight part of the S shape, still walking at a 45 degree angle but positioned so that you are parallel to his hind-quarters.

Move five The horse is now close to the centre line of the school and his head is still looking slightly to the left. Coil out several lengths of the left rein and move to the right (top photo).

Move six Walk forwards until you are walking just behind the horse on his right side. Coil up several lengths of the right rein. Ask him to look slightly to the right.

Move seven The horse has made the change of direction from the left to the right rein and you are moving on the second curve of the S shape (see the photo above).

Move eight Coil up several lengths of the right and left rein and walk at a 45 degree angle to the horse. He is now walking through the corner that originated the change of direction (see the photo below).

Move nine You have changed the rein on the move from the left to the right rein. Practise moves one to nine until you master each part and they flow into a continuous fluid movement. Be careful to be quick on your feet and stay with the movement of the horse. Always be safety conscious and never pass too close to his hindquarters.

If the horse is happily accepting the reins round his quarters and you are competently coiling the reins and changing the rein on the move, you are ready for Step 4.

STEP 4

Running the reins through the D rings The time has arrived to run the long reins through the D rings of the roller; the Ds stop the reins falling to the ground. This arrangement also gives an indirect rein effect which will help you to balance and frame the horse. Start by threading the inside rein through a D set high on the roller. The outside rein rests loosely on the horse's back.

PAUL'S TIP

It is very important not to get too close to the horse when you pass behind him. Remember, you could get kicked!

Once the horse accepts the outside rein willingly, you can progress to introducing the inside rein. Lunge the horse in walk and trot on the circle with the inside rein through the D and the outside rein through its D and resting over the horse's back. Continue working him on the circle and only when he is confident working on both reins, drive the horse forwards on straight lines.

The horse must take up a light, forward, supporting contact from your hand. A light contact is one that is comfortable for the horse; the horse should not pull against the contact nor feel 'strong' in the trainer's hands. To obtain a forward contact, drive the horse forward so that he takes up the supporting contact. The trainer's hands must allow the forward energy

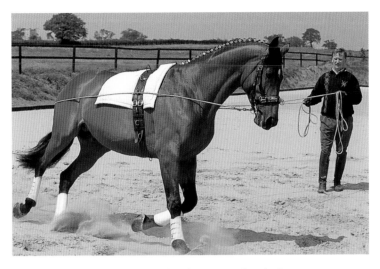

through the reins and, at the same time, maintain a 'connection' with the horse's mouth so that he steps forward actively to a light contact.

To achieve this, make sure you have a direct line from your elbows through your hands to the bit and that you hold the reins positively without pulling on the reins or restricting the horse in any way.

Driving the horse This helps to activate and straighten him. The inside rein acts where the rider's inside leg is normally held and the horse is driven to the outside rein, as with riding. This method of driving the horse makes it easy to teach turns and transitions. You can establish a better rhythm, contact and balance and the horse starts to develop more self-carriage.

Again, for safety's sake, do not walk too closely behind the horse because he could very quickly run backwards towards you.

In the early stages of driving the horse make sure he moves forwards briskly. Do not lag behind him so that you are pulling on the reins. Avoid this at all costs – it inhibits the horse's activity. Keep the contact light and go with the horse.

At first, you will need to jog when the horse is trotting but, after training, he should maintain a slow, energetic tempo that will enable you to keep up with his trot by striding out in walk.

The 45 degree angle This position gives you the opportunity to engage and drive the horse forwards more. It also allows you to maintain a safe distance from his hindquarters.

Engaging the hind leg Watch how the horse moves his hind legs. At the moment his outside hind leg is positioned further back than his inside one, send a flick down the outside rein. This has the effect of engaging the inside hind leg. This flick from the rein acts like a tap from a rider's leg and asks the horse to hold his inside leg further forward under his body. Because the rein is supported by the outside hind leg, it does not disturb the rein contact or the horse's mouth.

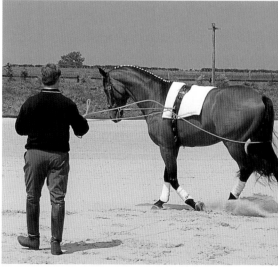

Flicking the inside rein

Again, watch the horse's hind legs. A second before he moves his inside hind leg forward, flick the inside rein against the horse's side at exactly the same place a rider would apply the inside leg aid. This flick is the equivalent to the leg aid. It is normally used when working on straight lines and helps keep the horse up to the outside rein.

Maintain a consistent contact on the outside rein.

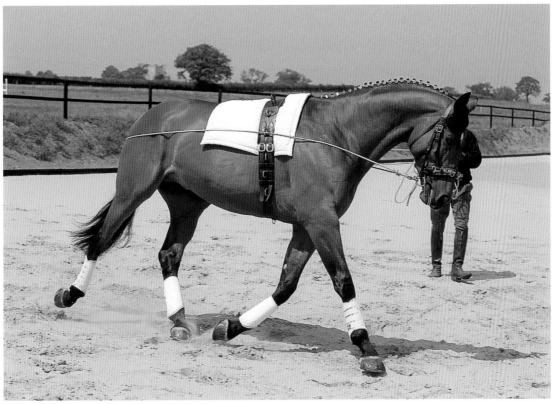

BALANCE

You can direct energy to:

a. Seek the bit. Ask the horse to move forward actively, in good rhythm and balance, and he will seek the bit. You are establishing the working gaits.

b. Contain the energy. This:
(**i**) re-directs a proportion of the energy to the hindquarters;
(**ii**) makes the horse step more 'up and under' his body;
(**iii**) lightens his forehand;
(**iv**) develops self-carriage.

TRANSITIONS

Transitions are the corner-stones of dressage. They teach the horse to differenti-ate between the different textures of the aids. For example, the horse has to develop the ability to differ-entiate between a contact that says frame yourself more and a contact that says allow the energy to move forward. Transitions improve the engagement and balance of the horse.

Long rein the horse in frequent transitions from trot to walk and canter to trot. Check that the horse moves forward briskly to the forward aids and responds to the half halts. Ensure he steps 'up and under' with his hindquarters in the downward transitions. This work confirms the horse has acquired a good understand-ing of the aids; it develops his attention and concentration.

Initially, ask for progressive transitions but when the horse develops in strength, make the transitions more frequent and more demanding, e.g. walk to canter.

HALF HALTS

Half halting contains the energy of the horse. Squeeze one or both reins (normally you half halt on the outside rein) or merely continue a consistent but slightly restrain-ing feel on one or both reins. This redirects a proportion of the horse's free forward movement back to his hindquarters and he becomes more engaged.

Initially, and to ensure you remain 'hand friendly' to the horse, use voice commands in conjunction with your hand commands.

RAISING THE FOREHAND

Firstly, you aim to teach the horse the aids and establish the working gaits. This im-proves the gaits: the horse stretches and loosens his muscles and becomes supple and relaxed enough to respond positively to the demands of increased engagement. Now you are in a position to ask the horse to raise his forehand. The horse's centre of gravity shifts, he carries more weight on his quarters and his gaits become more expressive.

PAUL'S TIP

Be wary of the dangers of overbending the horse. To understand what overbending means, imagine a line drawn from the horse's poll, through his nose to the ground. If his nose comes behind this imaginary line you know he is behind the vertical, or overbent. As an approximate guide, the novice horse should hold his nose 5–10 per cent in front of this vertical line and an advanced horse's nose should be 0–5 per cent in front of this line. Remember, the horse should be seeking the bit and not be pulled into a shape resem-bling flexion.

Horse moving in good novice outline. (above)
More engagement and higher head carriage (below and opposite page).

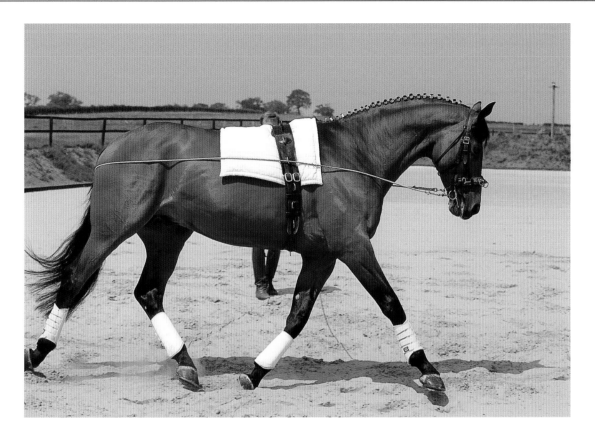

LONG REINING TO EDUCATE

The skilled trainer understands when to put the pressure on a horse and when to take the pressure off. For example, the educated hand maintains the horse's balance through the contact. This hand instructs and frames the horse sympathetically: it gives the contact when the horse gives a better feel on the reins and rebalances him when he takes too much weight on the reins. This understanding hand is proactive and not reactive.

First, you teach yourself to harmonize with the horse but, as you improve, you will be able to develop a more active role in training. Learn the tools of the trade, i.e. how the aids affect the horse's movement, and you can start to teach him. You will have progressed to being active with your influences. You will have learnt how to

PAUL'S TIP

Avoid artificially lifting the horse's head in the mistaken belief you are raising his forehand. The results can be disastrous: his back muscles collapse, his hindquarters spread out behind him, he becomes hollow backed. Engagement results in the horse lightening his forehand and raising his head and neck in a natural way.

achieve good results and you do this through consistency, repetition and intelligent observation.

Long reining allows you to practise training techniques without riding or upsetting the horse's balance. The horse should enjoy his long-reining work and be willing to respond happily to the trainer's requests.

STAYING WITH THE MOVEMENT

Stay with the movement of the horse, at all times and in all the gaits, this is essential for furthering the horse's long-rein training.

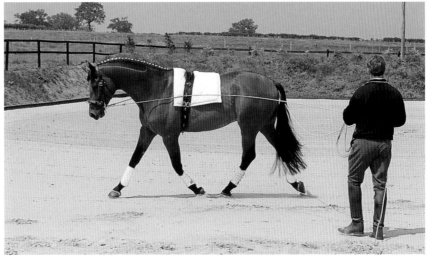

ACKNOWLEDGEMENTS

Thank you to Tessa Fielder for appearing in some of the photographs, to Maxine Spalding for her hard work as the groom and to the Selle Français stallion Broadland Baachuss. A special thank you to the late Lieutenant Colonel Bill Froud for his advice on long reining and expertise given to me over many years.

British Library Cataloguing-in-Publication Data.
A catalogue record for this book is available from the
British Library

ISBN 0.85131.733.2

Published in Great Britain in 1999 by
J. A. Allen & Company Limited,
1 Lower Grosvenor Place, Buckingham Palace Road,
London, SW1W OEL

Design and Typesetting by Paul Saunders
Series editor Jane Lake
Printed in Hong Kong by Dah Hua Printing Press Co. Ltd.